Things We Do!

CONTENTS

NATIONAL GEOGRAPHIC Hampton-Brown

School Publishing

Sounds for **f, n, l, p, c**

Listen to the beginning sounds.

Example:

fan

napkin

Lab

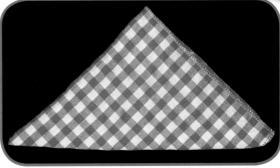

pan

cat

cap

High Frequency
Words

do
then
what
with
you
your

Key Words

Look at the picture.

Read the sentences.

What Do You Do?

1. **You** have a mat.

2. You have a cap.

3. **What** **do** you do **with** the mat?

4. **Then** what do you do with **your** cap?

What can you do with a cat?

Phonics Games
NGReach.com

3

Pat, Pat

by Lada Kratky

illustrated by Maurie Manning

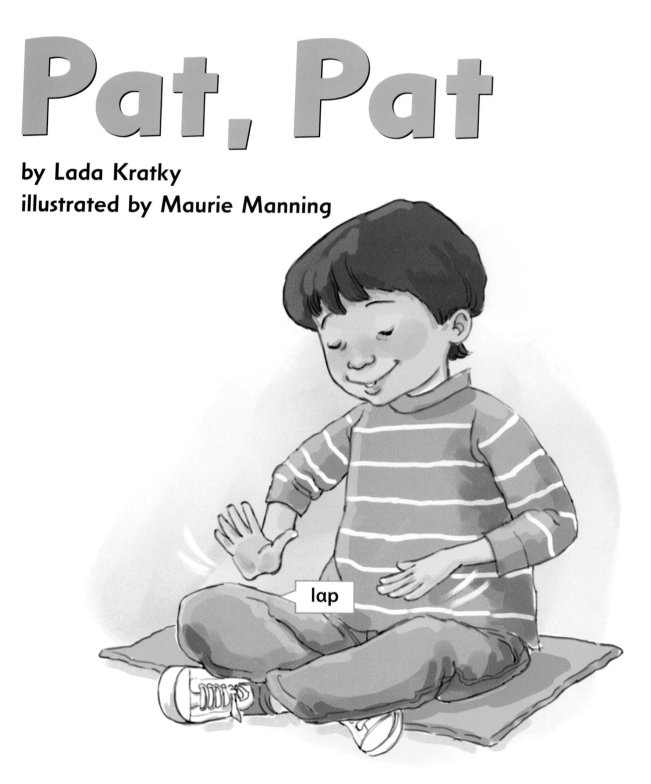

lap

Pat, pat, pat your lap.

cat

Pat, pat, pat your cat.

pan

Tap, tap, tap a pan.

can

Tap, tap, tap a can.

Fan, fan, fan with your hat.

Fan, fan, fan with your cap.

Then nap, nap, have a nap. ❖

Sounds for f, n, l, p, c

Read these words.

fan	nap	lap	cat
can	pan	pat	fat

Find the words that start with **f**.
Then find words that start with **n, l,
p,** and **c**. Use letters to build them.

f   a   n

Talk Together

Choose words from the box
above to tell your partner
what you see in the picture.

This is a can .

i

Words with Short i

Look at each picture. Read the words.

Example:

fin

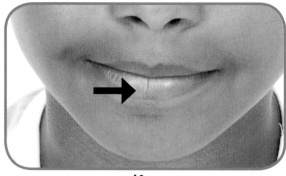

lip

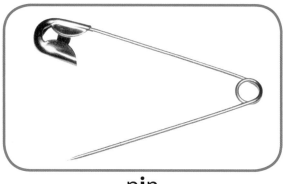

pin

sit

High Frequency
Words

do
then
what
with
you
your

Key Words

Read the sentences. Match each sentence to one of the pictures.

Pat Your Cat

1. **What** can **you** **do** **with** **your** cat?

2. You can pat your cat.

3. **Then** you can fan your cat.

Do you have a cat?

Phonics Games

NGReach.com

13

A Mat

by Lada Kratky

mat

What can you do with a mat?

You can sit on it.

mat

What can you do with a mat?

You can nap on it.

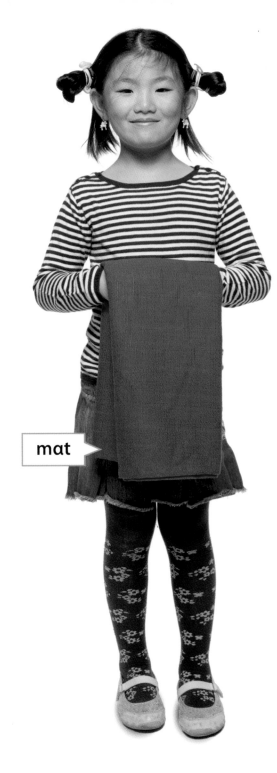

mat

What can you do with a mat?

You can sit on it and sip.

mat

What can you do with a mat? ❖

Words with Short i

Read these words.

sit	nap	sip	hat	Sis	Sam
it	hit	tip	lip	Pam	Tim

Find words with short **i**.
Use letters to build them.

s   i   t

Talk Together

Choose words from the box above to tell your partner what you see in the picture.

Sis can sip .

21

What Is It?

1 You can fan your cat with it.
Find it. What is it?

2 You can hit with it.
Find it. What is it?

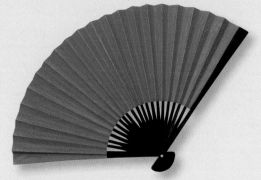

3 You can sip it. Find it. What is it?

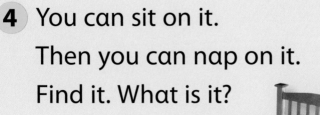

4 You can sit on it.
Then you can nap on it.
Find it. What is it?

Acknowledgments

Grateful acknowledgment is given to the authors, artists, photographers, museums, publishers, and agents for permission to reprint copyrighted material. Every effort has been made to secure the appropriate permission. If any omissions have been made or if corrections are required, please contact the Publisher.

Photographic Credits
CVR (Cover) Golden Pixels LLC/Alamy Images. **2** (bl) Gladkova Svetlana/Shutterstock. (br) Angelo Gilardelli/Shutterstock. (cl) Cpaquin/iStockphoto. (cr) R. Mackay Photography/ Shutterstock. (tl) Deepblue-Photographer/Shutterstock. (tr) Norma Zaro/iStockphoto. **3** (b) Liz Garza Williams/Hampton-Brown/National Geographic School Publishing. **11** (t) Liz Garza Williams/Hampton-Brown/National Geographic School Publishing. **12** (bl) Image Club. (br) Juniors Bildarchiv/age fotostock. (tl) senai aksoy/Shutterstock. (tr) Jaimie Duplass/ Shutterstock. **13** (b) Liz Garza Williams/Hampton-Brown/National Geographic School Publishing. **14** Mark Thiessen/Hampton-Brown/National Geographic School Publishing. **16** Mark Thiessen/Hampton-Brown/National Geographic School Publishing. **15** ©Azizur Rahim Peu/DrikNEWS/Majority World/The Image Works. **17** Juniors Bildarchiv/Alamy Images. **18** Mark Thiessen/Hampton-Brown/National Geographic School Publishing. **19** Cocoro Photos/ Corbis. **20** Julie Toy/Getty Images. **21** (t) Liz Garza Williams/Hampton-Brown/National Geographic School Publishing. **22** (bl) Supertrooper/Shutterstock. (br) Premier Edition Image Library/Superstock. (tl) ryasick/iStockphoto. (tr) PhotoDisc/Getty Images. **23** (bl) Corbis/age fotostock. (br) Stockbyte/Getty Images. (tl) Lorraine Kourafas/Shutterstock. (tr) Olga OSA/ Shutterstock.

Illustrator Credits
3, 11, 13, 21 Susan Reagan; **4-10** Maurie Manning

The National Geographic Society
John M. Fahey, Jr., President & Chief Executive Officer
Gilbert M. Grosvenor, Chairman of the Board

National Geographic School Publishing
Hampton-Brown
www.NGSP.com

Printed in the USA.
Quad Graphics, Leominster, MA

ISBN:978-0-7362-8023-5

18 19
10 9 8